Ultimate Friends Trivia Quiz: The One with All the Trivia

F·R·I·E·N·D·S

Copyright Declaration

Copyright © 2020 by Rain Publishing

All rights reserved. No
part of this book
may be reproduced
or used in any
manner without
written permission
of the copyright
owner except for the
use of quotations in
a book review.

First Edition June 2020

Book design by Donald Blake
Cover design by V. Rain

Other Books from from the Author

For more such interesting behind the screen and on-screen facts and stories. Check out other popular TV Trivia Books from the Author.

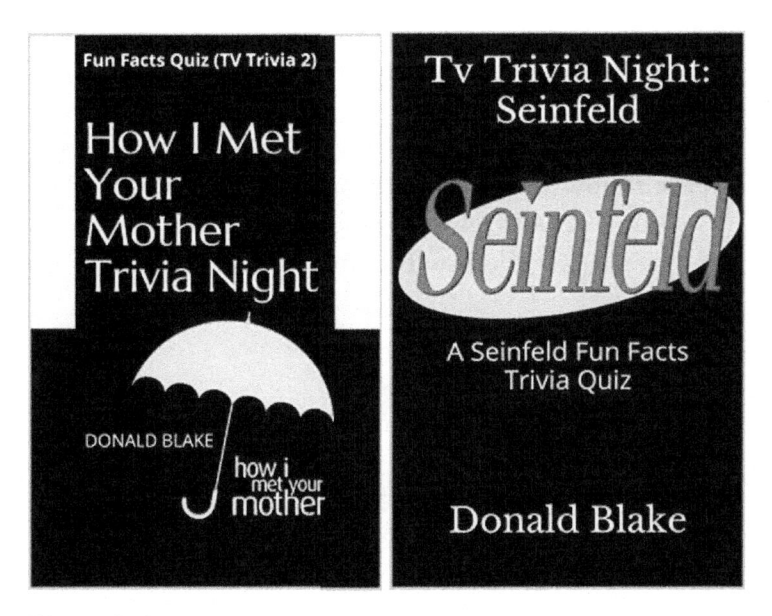

Links Below:

https://www.amazon.com/dp/109555509X

https://www.amazon.com/dp/165228723X

To subscribe to our future releases

Please follow Donald Blake on Amazon the book details page by clicking on the 'Follow Button'

Follow the Author

Sir Donald Blake ✓ Following

You can also mail us at

donaldblake.trivia@gmail.com

to get yourself added to our mailing list.

Contents

Introduction: 7
The One About Season-1: Set-1 8
Answers: 11
The One About Season-1: Set-2 12
Answers: 14
The One About Season-2: Set-1 15
Answers: 17
The One About Season-2: Set-2 18
Answers: 20
The One About Season-3: Set-1 21
Answers: 23
The One About Season-3: Set-2 24
Answers: 26
The One About Season-4: Set-1 27
Answers: 29
The One About Season-4: Set-2 30
Answers: 32
The One About Season-5: Set-1 33
Answers: 35
The One About Season 5: Set-2 36
Answers: 38

The One About Season-6: Set-1 39
Answers: 41
The One About Season-6: Set-2 42
Answers: 44
The One About Season-7: Set-1 45
Answers: 47
The One About Season-7: Set-2 48
Answers: 50
The One About Season-8: Set-1 51
Answers: 53
The One About Season-8: Set-2 54
Answers: 57
The One About Season-9: Set-1 58
Answers: 60
The One About Season-9: Set-2 61
Answers: 63
The One About Season-10: Set-1 64
Answers: 66
The One About Season-10: Set-2 67
Answers: 70

Introduction:

How you doin'?

This is the **2nd book** in our **FRIENDs Trivia Series** containing over **500 questions** covering **all the 10 seasons** of our beloved and trans-generational TV show **F.R.I.E.N.D.S** which has had a tremendous cultural impact across the globe. A show that everybody relates to, no matter which country or culture they might belong to.

In this volume, the questions are chronologically arranged and carefully curated and designed to make you rack your brain and remember and relive all fun moments of the show all over again right from the beginning to end.

We have dedicated two sets to each seasons. **One set contains 25 questions.**

The first book in the series is a hard-core fan's dream come true. A lot of hard work has been put to research and collate all the interesting behind the scenes stories, trivia about the actors and fun facts about all the set-pieces & references used in the show all in one book.

All the best before you embark on this journey. Have fun and score high!

The One About Season-1: Set-1

1. What is the name Ross & Monica's Childhood pet whose death had been hidden from them by their parents?

2. What is the name of Carol's lesbian partner?

3. Which profession was Rachel's fiancé Barry in?

4. Whose babies does Rachel curse by saying "I just hope they have his old hairline and your old nose!"?

5. Whose name was inspired by a name tag on a janitor's uniform worn by Phoebe?

6. Who first accidentally reveals to Rachel that Ross is in love with her?

7. Who gifts Rachel a cameo that looked like just the one that belonged to her grandmother?

8. Which girlfriend of Ross played by Lauren Tom was sabotaged by Rachel multiple times by asking Phoebe to give her a terrible haircut and stalling her from consummating her relationship with Ross?

9. Phoebe learns that an extra 500$ has been added to her bank account. She wasn't able to use the money because of the guilt. What did she get from the bank when she reported the incident to the bank?

10. Why did Phoebe receive a compensation of 7000$ from a soda company?

11. Monica's friends had always mocked her boyfriends. Name the one boyfriend who was a hit with her friends?

12. Which part of the New York state was Rachel originally from?

13. What was Ross hit in the face with during the Rangers game forcing him to go to an emergency room?

14. Rachel was upset about her low income, her old friends' success and happiness and how her life is falling apart in general, starts drinking this drink directly from the Blender on learning that it contains Rum. What was the name of the drink?

15. After the delivery boy mistakenly exchanges the girls' pizza with a neighbor, the girls get interested and start spying on him & his date through a pair of binoculars. What was the name of the neighbor who also lend his name to the episode?

16. Who did Phoebe give the money & the phone from the bank?

17. What did Rachel's father promise her if she decides to move back home?

18. *Uberweiss!* "It's new, it's German, it's extra-tough". What was Ross talking about?

19. What was the first Job that *Estelle Leonard Talent Agency* get Joey?

20. Name the musical based on an Austrian neurologist and the founder of psychoanalysis, a clinical method for treating psychopathology, whose character was played by Joey.

21. Name the exotic woman Chandler meets at Joey's Musical who is not only married to a guy named Rick, but also has a boyfriend called Ethan. Nonetheless, she still wanted to see Chandler for sexual reasons alone.

22. Name the Supermodel with whom Chandler was trapped in the ATM.

23. Name the "The Weird Man" who often complained about the noise that Monica & Rachel made by tapping on his apartment ceiling with a broom.

24. Ross is extremely jealous of the Italian hunk Paolo and makes fun of him behind his back every chance he gets. Taking advantage of the fact that Paolo speaks little English what does Ross call him on his face?

25. Rachel says "Yeah, but then you spent Phoebe's *entire* birthday party talking to my breasts, so then I figured maybe not". What did Rachel figure and about whom?

Answers:

1. Chi Chi
2. Susan
3. Orthodontist
4. Mindy
5. Ben
6. Chandler
7. Ross
8. Julie
9. A Football phone
10. Human thumb in the Soda Can
11. Alan
12. Long Island
13. The hockey puck
14. Tiki Death Punch
15. George Stephanopoulos
16. Lizzy, a homeless friend
17. Mercedes Convertible
18. Ross's favorite laundry detergent
19. Al Pacino's butt double
20. Freud!
21. Aurora
22. Jill Goodacre
23. Mr. Heckles
24. "crap weasel"
25. That Chandler may not be gay

The One About Season-1: Set-2

1. Which Character wants to get buried at the sea to prove to people he isn't that predictable as people thought?

2. When the Thanksgiving dinner is burned and Rachel misses her flight. What does everyone ends up eating?

3. Joey wants to have dinner with family but ends up having dinner at Monica's. Why was he too embarrassed to go home on Thanksgiving?

4. Why does Phoebe celebrate two Thanksgivings?

5. What did everyone rush to watch locking themselves out on the roof on the Thanksgiving without a key?

6. What pact made by everyone for the New Years Eve Party was ultimately broken by everybody?

7. Which friend kisses Chandler's mom?

8. Who said this "Oh no, I am a fabulous mom! I bought my son his first condom"?

9. Inspired by Chandler's Mom, Rachel starts writing a book but turns out she is not a very good typist. What is the name of the Book?

10. Chandler's mother appeared as a guest on a talk show, which he is uncomfortable watching due to his mother's more-than-embarrassing remarks. Which real show did she appear in?

11. Which friend made the best oatmeal-raisin cookies in the world?

12. When Joey and Chandler couldn't agree on a new table they wanted to buy, what did they end up buying instead?

13. According to Chandler's Mom, what do you get when you "start with half a dozen European cities, throw in thirty euphemisms for male genitalia!"?

14. Phoebe's new boyfriend, Roger, depresses and angers everyone. Which profession was he into?

15. Who had been having an affair with a woman named Ronni, a pet mortician, for six years?

16. Phoebe, Monica, and Rachel have a cleansing ritual, which turns into a small fire; The Firemen came to the rescue. What were they trying to "cleanse"?

17. Name Joey's sister who couldn't see her husband anymore because of a restraining order he got.

18. Ross goes out with Celia, a woman from the museum, who wants him for something; a skill he wasn't great at... at first. What did she want Ross to do?

19. Who switched Monica's TV into Spanish mode? And No one could figure out how to switch it back.

20. What was Joey's family business that he didn't want to be a part of?

21. Who ends up hanging upside down outside Mr. Heckles' window while taking down the Christmas lights?

22. Whose choking on scrabble tiles and subsequent hospitalization make Ross realize that he can cope with the responsibilities of parenthood?

23. Rachel, tired of being a waitress, sends out her resumes. Which fashion store did she get her first interview call from?

24. What was the misspelled word on Rachel's resume?

25. When Joey is thinking of a name that's more neutral. What 'neutral' name change does Chandler suggest Joey?

Answers:

1. Jack Geller
2. Chandler's cheese sandwiches and Funyuns for Dinner.
3. Because of the VD poster featuring him
4. One with Her grandmother's boyfriend, who uses a lunar calendar, and one with Monica on actual Thanksgiving.
5. The Underdog balloon that has escaped the Thanksgiving Day parade
6. No-Date Pact
7. Ross
8. Mrs. Bing – Chandler's Mother
9. A Woman Undone
10. The Tonight Show with Jay Leno
11. Phoebe
12. The foosball table
13. A Romance Novel
14. A psychiatrist
15. Joey's Dad
16. Bad luck with men
17. Tina
18. Talk dirty
19. Marcel
20. Pipe-fitting Business
21. Rachel
22. Marcel
23. Saks fifth Avenue
24. Compuper
25. Joey to Joseph Stalin

The One About Season-2: Set-1

1. Monica went shopping with Ross's girlfriend Julie. Not just the activity but the choice of the store they went to makes Rachel feel betrayed. Where had they gone shopping?

2. Name Joey's inappropriate tailor who grabs Chandler by his crotch and is labeled as a "very bad man" by him.

3. Julie wanted an Andie MacDowell haircut. When Phoebe asks Rachel, how Andie MacDowell wears her hair. Who did Rachel say Andie MacDowell was?

4. Who threatens Joey's Status as a Bijan cologne Man and steals his potential date, Annabelle, from him?

5. What did Ross eat with Carol's Breast Milk?

6. After clearing Mr. Heckles room, Chandler finds out that he shares something in common with Mr. Heckles and keeps a souvenir. What item did he choose to keep from all his possessions?

7. Name the Hollywood beauty who plays Erika, a crazed *Days of our lives* fan who stalked and dated Joey.

8. Why was Phoebe married to her "gay" friend Duncan, who later turned out to be heterosexual?

9. Whose underwear was stuck on the telephone pole outside the apartment?

10. According to Chandler, pressing which part of his body opens the delivery entrance to the magical land of Narnia?

11. Chandler reveals that Joey was in a porn movie. What role did Joey play in the porn movie?

12. Monica was fired from her Job as Head Lunch Chef for accepting a gift from the Restaurant's new meat supplier. What was the gift or alleged kickback?

13. Name the intriguing woman who kept calling Chandler looking for someone named "Bob"?

14. What did Ross do to choose between Julie & Rachel?

15. Why do Rachel & Monica receive mangled papers and smashed packages during Christmas?

16. Chandler was planning Ross's birthday, involving a gift, a cake, and tickets to see a concert with an expensive ticket which causes a rife between the friends. Whose concert did they go to?

17. When Joey and Chandler lose the baby and later Chandler changes Ben's diaper, what does he sees written on Ben's butt?

18. Which movie star asks out Rachel when she was trying to get him interested in Monica?

19. What phrase was being used by people in the party to refer to Richard Burke's young new girlfriend (Monica) at Jack Geller's Party?

20. Phoebe's Navy man was in town for two weeks, but their plans were foiled because Phoebe wasn't well. What was Phoebe suffering from?

21. What Job does Chandler get Joey at his office?

22. While working at Chandler's office Joey invents a character who has a wife that Chandler slept with and two little girls Brittany and Ashley, and a third on the way. What is the name of the character?

23. Which character is turned on by uniforms?

24. Who was the maid of Honor for Mindy's wedding with Barry?

25. Rachel had left Barry on the altar and appeared at his wedding with her dress caught in her underwear. Which disease did Barry's parents tell everyone she is insane from?

Answers:

1. Bloomingdales
2. Frankie
3. "The guy from Planet of the Apes"
4. The Hombre Man
5. Half-a-dozen Oreo Cookies
6. Mr. Heckles Yearbook
7. Brooke Sheilds
8. For Green Card
9. Monica's
10. His third Nipple
11. Trying to fix a copier
12. Five Steaks & an Eggplant
13. Jade
14. A list of pros & cons
15. Made cookies to give instead of cash as holiday tips
16. Hootie and the Blowfish
17. "Property of Human Services"
18. Jean-Claude Van Damme
19. "New twinkie in the city"
20. Phoebe has chicken-pox
21. His Processor
22. Joseph the processing guy
23. Rachel
24. Rachel
25. Syphilis

The One About Season-2: Set-2

1. Ross plays Marcel's favorite song to get Marcel's attention when he is on the set of the Outbreak movie. Which song does he play?

2. After the girls realize that they are out of condoms, except for the last one lying around. The girls flip a coin to see who will get the last one. Who won?

3. How do we know "Terry", a character portrayed by Max Wright?

4. What was the secret behind fun bobby being so 'fun'?

5. When Joey starts earning some money he gives Chandler an expensive gift that Chandler refers as a "reject from the Mr. T collection". What did he gift Chandler?

6. In which commercial does Ross spot a familiar looking monkey that reminds him of Marcel, his pet monkey?

7. When planning for their future where does Ross say he and Rachel will live and raise their family?

8. Who was obsessed with his ex-girlfriend and accused Chandler of sleeping with her, and killing the fish he bought for him?

9. Chandler bumps into the movie set who knew her in the fourth grade and was embarrassed by lifting her skirt during the class play. What nickname had she earned because of this incident?

10. Who makes a guest appearance as Susie Moss?

11. How does Susie Moss get back at Chandler?

12. Ross and Rachel's heated argument quickly turns into a passionate first kiss in the rain. Where did they first kiss?

13. According to Phoebe, as explained to Ross Geller, which crustaceans are the most devoted, loyal species on the planet that can be seen walking alongside each other holding hands?

14. The show writers in Days of Our Lives kill Joey's character Dr. Ramoray by making him fall down an elevator shaft. What did he do to piss off the writers?

15. Name the 1950's themed diner where Monica takes up a job as a waitress and wears blond wig, roller skates and fake breasts.

16. What was Richard Burke's Profession?

17. Rachel starts dating Ross's doppelganger 'Russ'. Russ's job was something very similar to what Ross did for a living. What was his occupation?

18. Tired of selling her soul in 50's themed diner, Monica invests in a stock with ticker symbol MEG. What was the stock choice based on?

19. What was Rachel's fiancé Barry Faber's profession?

20. Stephanie Schiffer is the girl Terry hired in season 2 to sing in Central Perk, causing resentment by Phoebe. Which rock legend made a guest appearance as Stephanie?

21. In Ross' list Rachel flaws were listed as "spoiled, ditzy, too much into her looks, and just a waitress" - but what was listed as one flaw under Julie?

22. Monica used a synthetic chocolate substitute that disgusts Rachel and Phoebe so much so that after eating it Phoebe described it as "what evil must taste like". What was it called?

23. Who does duplicate Ross, Russ end up dating right after noticing her at the coffeehouse?

24. Which part was played by Joey in the show *Days of our lives*?

25. Whose spirit which wanted to "see everything" had possessed Phoebe's body?

Answers:

1. The Lion Sleeps Tonight
2. Rachel
3. Owner & Manager of Central Perk
4. He was drunk all the time.
5. A gold bracelet
6. The Monkeyshine Beer
7. Scarsdale
8. Chandler's new roommate Eddie.
9. Susie "Underpants" Moss
10. Julia Roberts
11. She left him naked wearing pink panties
12. At Central Perk
13. Lobsters
14. Joey's claims in Soap Opera Digest that he writes a lot of his own lines
15. Moondance
16. Ophthalmologist
17. Periodontist
18. Her Initials
19. Orthodontist
20. Chrissie Hyde of The Pretenders.
21. "She's not Rachel"
22. Mockolate
23. Julie
24. Dr. Drake Ramoray
25. Mrs. Adelman

The One About Season-3: Set-1

1. Who does Rachel exactly dress as in a golden color bikini to fulfill Ross's fantasy?

2. What is the name of the maneuver designed by Ross to end the cuddling and give you some space?

3. What happens when Chandler tries Ross's secret maneuver to 'de-cuddle'?

4. Which toy that Ben likes playing with didn't make sense for Ross?

5. In the episode, "The one with Frank Jr." the gang considers what five celebrities would be on their "freebie list". What is a "freebie list"?

6. Who was on top of Ross' Freebie list?

7. Which celebrity eliminated by Ross from his list unfortunately, bumps into him?

8. What does Joey ends up building when he gets a little carried away by a mailbox project?

9. What is the name of the acting class that Joey teaches?

10. Ross's meeting with Rachel's father wasn't going well but then they eventually found something to bond over. What?

11. Why does Phoebe avoid going to the dentist?

12. In the third season thanksgiving, all six decide to play football together. What cup did Monica and Ross compete for?

13. Who flashes the other team during the football match to score?

14. Ross ends up accidentally breaking a little girl's leg. What does he then had to sell for her so she can go to Space Camp.?

15. Who starts working at a Christmas Tree lot in season Three?

16. What is the name of the busboy that Monica dated while working in the 50's themed restaurant, Moon dance Diner?

17. Name the poem written by Monica's diner co-worker which is is later revealed that it is in fact in contempt for all women.

18. Phoebe starts dating a Jock named Robert. Why does his presence make the group uncomfortable?

19. What was revealed to be Joey's favorite book?

20. Which book did Rachel give Joey to read when they exchange their favorite books?

21. Who does Leslie (Phoebe's former music partner) sell "Smelly Cat" to?

22. Chandler meets a girl named Ginger at Central Perk. It was later revealed that Joey had dated her earlier and did a horrible thing. What did Joey do when they were dating?

23. Although, Chandler was freaked out to learn that Ginger had an artificial leg, it was ginger who broke up with Chandler. Why?

24. What does Chandler suspect could be responsible for the loss of his all (joking) powers?

25. Which person did Rachel and Ross fight over leading to the "break"?

Answers:

1. Princess Leia
2. "hug and roll"
3. Janice falls on the floor
4. A Barbie doll
5. People they can sleep with without anyone getting upset
6. Uma Thurman
7. Isabella Rossellini
8. The entertainment center
9. Acting for Soap Operas
10. Rachel's flaws
11. Whenever she goes, someone dies
12. The "Geller Cup."
13. Phoebe
14. Brown Bird Cookies
15. Joey
16. Julio
17. The Empty Vase
18. His shorts are a little too revealing
19. The Shining
20. The little Women
21. Kitty litter Company
22. Joey accidentally threw Ginger's artificial leg onto a fire
23. Because of Chandler's "Nubbin"
24. Nubbinectomy.
25. Mark

The One About Season-3: Set-2

1. What was the name of the girl who invites Joey and Chandler to a dance club but ends up sleeping with Ross?
2. Chandler starts smoking again under the stress of Rachel & Ross breaking up. What does Rachel give Chandler to help him quit smoking?
3. What subject did Frank Jr.'s old wife teach in his school?
4. At the Diner, Monica meets a millionaire who is said to have invented Moss 865 and runs a large computer corporation. Name him.
5. Where did Monica's Millionaire date take her on the first date to have pizza?
6. Monica's millionaire boyfriend was a high achiever but he abysmally failed at this particular sport he was insanely obsessed with. Monica couldn't see the pain and eventually broke up with him. What sports was Pete into?
7. Rachel wanted to return some of Ross's stuff but he gets upset and demands all his stuff back, which special item dear to Rachel was included in "all his stuff"?
8. What does Monica's Aunt Silvia leave when she passes away?
9. From which doll room did the fire originated in Phoebe's dollhouse?
10. Whose new boss has a habit of slapping him/her on the behind?
11. Name the shaved head girl Phoebe sets Ross up with approval from Rachel who later finds out that she now has plenty of hair and looks beautiful.
12. By what nickname does Rachel's father call Ross?
13. Janice ex-husband owned a mattress company. What was her husband called?

14. According to Rachel what do regulars who don't tip well get served?

15. What does Joey do to convey 'confusion' in scene when he had just received bad news?

16. Which role did Joey and his student get an audition for in "All My children"?

17. Who claims that his/her right leg is two inches shorter than the right leg?

18. What did get mistakenly delivered instead of a mattress while Phoebe was busy attending to Joey's bleeding nose?

19. What was the giant poking device used to poke & check the Ugly Naked Guy, made of?

20. Where does Joey keep his copy of The Shining when he isn't reading it?

21. Wheat is Ross' favorite song?

22. How much did Pete Becker tip Monica with a check which had his number written on back of it?

23. What's written on the Ross's tiny t-shirt that Rachel loves?

24. Ross has a weird skin condition that nobody seems to identify until he visits Phoebe's herbalist, Guru Saj, who successfully removes it - by catching it on his watch while making a hand gesture. What did he identify the condition as?

25. Who was Phoebe's birth mother?

Answers:

1. Chloe
2. Hypnosis tape
3. Home Economics
4. Pete Becker
5. Italy
6. UFC
7. A tiny t-shirt
8. A beautiful dollhouse to Monica
9. In the Aroma Room
10. Chandler
11. Bonnie
12. "Wet Head"
13. Mattress king
14. Sneezers
15. He starts dividing 232/13
16. Nick the Boxer
17. Rachel
18. Race car bed
19. Chop-sticks
20. The Freezer
21. U2's With Or Without You
22. $20,000
23. "Frankie says Relax"
24. "Koondis"
25. Phoebe Abbot

The One About Season-4: Set-1

1. Who peed on Monica to ease the pain from the Jellyfish string?
2. What does Phoebe think her mother reincarnated as?
3. What do Joey & Chandler exchange their entertainment center for?
4. What does Monica lose in one of the quiches that she prepared while catering for her mother's party?
5. As joey doesn't have enough money to buy the entire encyclopedia set all starting with a letter, he buys just one book. The letter volume was it?
6. What did Joey had to teach Mr. Treeger to smooth things out with him?
7. Phoebe struggles to contain her desires for someone named Rick who ultimately turns out to be married. Where did she meet Rick?
8. While Gunther couldn't get a kiss from Rachel, he definitely did get one from Phoebe. Why does phoebe kiss Gunther?
9. Why does Phoebe wanted to catch another cold?
10. Rachel dates a 'dude' named Josh, a college soccer player to show off Ross. Why did Rachel break up with him eventually?
11. Name Rachel's ex who Monica starts dating in *The One With the Cat*.
12. Chandler buys a rare copy of Kathy's favorite book for her birthday. Which book?
13. While Chandler gets Kathy a very thoughtful gift, what does Joey buy her?

14. Ross finds Cheryl, an undeniably beautiful doctoral paleontology candidate who unfortunately she lacks a fundamental quality. Why does Ross break up with her?

15. How is Chandler punished for kissing Kathy and betraying Joey?

16. When Monica injures her eye, she arranges to see the on-call doctor, who turns out to be very cute. Who was he related to?

17. How did Monica get an eyepatch?

18. What did Ross and Chandler call their party wizard friend, a reference to famous wizard with similar characteristics from "Lord of the rings"?

19. Monica fills in for a food critic and gives a bad review to this restaurant and was ultimately hired as its head chef. Which restaurant in the show are we talking about?

20. Joana sabotages Rachel's interview for which position?

21. Ross meets an amazing girl on the train, whom he finds really beautiful, smart and funny but the only problem was she lived very far. Where was the girl from?

22. After Bloomingdale's closes down Rachel's department to what position is Rachel demoted to?

23. Chandler couldn't get rid of Janice, hence, lies about going to another country for work. Which country does he say he is travelling to?

24. What sports does Ross play with Emily's friends Liam and Devon?

25. Where does Ross end up when he takes a train to Poughkeepsie to break up and falls asleep?

Answers:

1. Chandler
2. As a cat
3. A Canoe
4. A fake nail
5. V
6. Ball room Dancing
7. Rick, one of her massage clients
8. To catch another cold
9. Because it made her sound sexy
10. He starts stealing form her
11. Chip Douglas
12. The Velveteen Rabbit
13. A pen (which is also a clock).
14. She was a slob
15. By spending the Thanksgiving Day in a box.
16. Richard's son Timothy
17. she chips at some ice that hits her eye
18. Gandalf
19. Alessandro's
20. Assistant Buyer
21. from Poughkeepsie
22. Personal Shopper
23. Yemen
24. Rugby
25. Montreal

The One About Season-4: Set-2

1. Who does Rachel tries to impress by putting on her old high school uniform for?

2. After a tie in the Trivia quiz, the money wasn't enough, the stakes flew high. What did the girls ask Joey and Chandler to get rid of if they lose?

3. What did the girls offer the first time to persuade Joey and Chandler to get back their apartment back to which Joe agrees but Chandler doesn't?

4. The girls had swapped the apartments when the guys were away, Chandler feels cheated and tries to reclaim the apartment by menacingly accusing the girls of stealing it. What do the girls offer the guys to which they later called as "totally worth it"?

5. The girls' decision to leave Joey & Chandler's apartment was triggered by their neighbor who woke them up every morning by singing a song? Which song did the neighbor sing in the morning?

6. Although Chandler's friends have no clue about what he does during the contest for the apartment, Rachel takes a shot at guessing his job title. What does she guess?

7. When Phoebe's brother Frank learns that he is going to have triplets. He decides to quit college. Which college did he go to?

8. Rachel plans a big date with a special dinner, new lingerie and a nice dress what upsets Joshua while eating dinner at her place?

9. What does Chandler accidentally reveal to Ross as his middle name?

10. Who was initially chosen as Ross's best man for his wedding with Emily?

11. Joey's loses Ross's ring and everyone suspects the stripper but she didn't have it. Who was the real culprit?

12. Which celebrity does Joey meet while in London for Ross's wedding?

13. Under what name did Phoebe call Emily's mother as Ross's doctor to explain why he mixed up the names?

14. Who persuaded Ross to get his ear pierced spontaneously?

15. According to Monica, How many erogenous zones are there in the female body?

16. Which magazine gave Monica an opportunity to fill in as a food critic?

17. What was the first baby name that came to Phoebe's mind when they are deciding on the baby names for Phoebe's unborn children?

18. What had Monica's parents turned Monica's childhood bedroom into?

19. With his ears pierced which rock star does Ross compare himself to?

20. Which household chore does Rachel keep ignoring and putting off?

21. What was Joey's nickname at Allesandro's?

22. When Phoebe was having contractions, Monica asks Rachel to get the book. Though she was referring to a pregnancy book, what book did Rachel get her?

23. Why couldn't Ross play and hurt himself while playing badminton with Rachel's father?

24. Which TV show with lot of slow-motion scenes did Chandler and Joey often watch? Mathew Perry even dated the actor, Yasmin Bleeth, from this show.

25. Name the famous actor who made an unscripted cameo in the beginning of episode "The one with the Ultimate Fighting Champion".

Answers:

1. Joshua
2. The duck and the rooster
3. Season tickets for the Knicks
4. The girls offer to kiss each other for one minute
5. "Morning's Here"
6. "Transponster"
7. Refrigerator College
8. the chick and the duck
9. Muriel
10. Joey
11. The Duck
12. Fergie
13. Dr. Phalange
14. Emily
15. Seven
16. The Chelsea Reporter
17. Cougar
18. A Gym
19. David Bowie
20. Washing dishes
21. Dragon
22. A Bible
23. Their Dog kept staring at him
24. Baywatch
25. Robin Williams

The One About Season-5: Set-1

1. Which character decides to outsource her decision making control to Monica?

2. What was Joey's kidney stone initially perceived as?

3. Phoebe gave birth to two girls and a boy. What was the name of the second baby girl?

4. When Phoebe gets her first contraction, Joey is struck with a pain for worse which Phoebe suspects as 'sympathy pains'. What was the real reason behind Joey's pain?

5. Phoebe is annoyed with her replacement doctor Dr. Harad who seems to like a certain TV character and even demands that Ross should go find her a different doctor. Which TV character was the good doctor fond of?

6. To make herself feel a little better, which TV show did Phoebe write letter to after her mom committed suicide but never received a reply?

7. What was the name of Rachel's Dog?

8. When Emily asks Ross not to see Rachel, Ross equates her to Chandler's former roommate who dated Monica and got "phased out" of the group after a messy breakup. Who did Ross feared that Rachel would become the next version of?

9. Phoebe hates PBS, because they never replied to her letters she wrote but sent her something instead of a letter. What did they send her instead?

10. What does Phoebe receive as a family heirloom from her grandmother?

11. Rachel & Monica stumble upon a scary looking man with a wild beard with a pickaxe in the storage room whom they call "a beast man", "a yeti". Who was it actually?

12. Phoebe starts dating Larry as she is turned on by his power to close places down. What did Larry do for a living?

13. How did Phoebe lose an arm (twice) in past lives' (1862 and 1915) thanksgivings?

14. Monica tries to make Chandler take his clothes off by rubbing things on her body in an attempt to seduce him but unfortunately ends up severing chandler's toe. What did she drop on him?

15. What did Rachel start comparing Jane Eyre to in the English class with Phoebe?

16. What does Ross call the extra slice of gravy-soaked bread in the middle of the thanks-giving sandwich?

17. Who had been eating Ross's sandwiches all along and triggering Ross's anger?

18. Ross persuades Joey to write a film to branch out on his film career. After penning a few words, he gives up and becomes distracted by a game. What was the name of this very dangerous game invented by Joey & Chandler?

19. Why does Rachel Break up with Danny?

20. In "The One with All the Resolutions", everyone discusses their resolutions. While Ross' resolution is to be happy in 1999, what was Phoebe's resolution? .

21. What reason did Janice give for breaking up with Ross?

22. Why did Ursula skip their grandmother's memorial?

23. Who was an unexpected guest at the Phoebe-Grandmother's funeral?

24. How did Ross get the Ugly naked guy's apartment?

25. Ironically, while packing up what were most of Ugly Naked Guy's boxes labeled as?

Answers:
1. Rachel
2. Sympathy Pains
3. Chandler
4. Kidney Stones
5. Fonzie from Happy days
6. Sesame Street
7. LaPooh
8. The next Kip
9. A keychain
10. A mink coat
11. Their New Neighbor Danny
12. Health inspector
13. In the war
14. Kitchen knife
15. A cyborg
16. The moist maker
17. Ross's Boss
18. Fireball
19. Because of his inappropriate sister Krista
20. Pilot a commercial jet
21. Ross whines a lot
22. She thought grandmother was already dead
23. Phoebe's father
24. By getting Naked
25. Clothes (Underwear, shoes etc.)

The One About Season 5: Set-2

1. From where did Phoebe see Chandler & Monica "doing it", thus revealing their little secret?

2. Who was the last one to find about "Chandler & Monica"?

3. What is the name of Joey's bedtime penguin pal?

4. There's too much competition for Ugly Naked Guy's apartment and a lot of people had sent him expensive gifts. What did Ross send to bribe him?

5. How does Ugly Naked Guys' cat die?

6. Everyone in the new building decides Ross is cheap and not "their kind of people" when he doesn't pay 100 dollars to the tenant's committee. What was the 100 dollars for?

7. What does Phoebe use the NYPD badge she finds in a wallet in the coffeehouse for?

8. When Phoebe uses a NYPD badge against the cop it belongs to, the cop is charmed by her and they start dating. What was the name of the sweet cop?

9. What word was used by Ross to repeatedly instruct Chandler and Rachel while moving the couch upstairs to his apartment?

10. Rachel did something so awkward with her interviewer Mr. Zelner that she thought that she had blown her Job prospects with Ralph Lauren. What did she do?

11. What was the new reason for misunderstanding between Rachel in her second interview with Mr.Zelner for Ralph Lauren?

12. Ross is excited when he gets Jen's number, a beautiful blond girl who agrees that he was unfairly treated by the tenant's committee. How do we better know Jen?

13. What inappropriate thing did Rachel accidentally do in her final interview with Mr.Zelner?

14. What was Phoebe put in charge of for Rachel's surprise birthday party?

15. What food commercial were Ben and Joey competing for?

16. What does Joey keep telling instead of just 'soup' in the soup commercial?

17. What did Phoebe decorate Rachel's birthday with to teach Monica a lesson?

18. Joey's Grandma comes to Monica's apartment to watch his big scene in her favourite show but he was unfortunately cut from it. Which show?

19. Gary, the sweet cop had a good going with Phoebe, they even moved in together. Why does phoebe break up with him?

20. Rachel pays an obscenely exorbitant price for an unusual hairless weird cat that freaks out her friends. What was the reason behind it?

21. What was the name of Rachel's hairless cat that everyone hated?

22. Who buys Rachel weird cat for Mrs. Whiskerson for $1500?

23. Name the movie in which Joey gets offered the lead role in an independent film, getting shot in Las Vegas.

24. How does Joey makes his ends meet when the movie where he was promised a lead role was shut down?

25. Joey decides to turn a $100 tip into money he needs finish his movie. Although, he losses, he discover something far more valuable (to him). What did he find in the Casino?

Answers:

1. Ugly Naked guys apartment
2. Ross
3. Huggsy
4. A small basket of Mini Muffins
5. He sat on it
6. For the retiring Handyman's gift
7. For saving nature
8. Gary
9. Pivot
10. She kissed him
11. Ink on her lips
12. Joey' "Hot Girl"
13. Touched his Penis
14. Cups and Ice
15. A soup commercial
16. Noodle Soup
17. With Cups
18. Law & Order
19. He shot a bird
20. Her grandmother had a cat like that when she was a kid
21. Mrs. Whiskerson
22. Gunther
23. Shutter Speed
24. As a gladiator at Caesar's Palace.
25. His Hand twin

\

The One About Season-6: Set-1

1. What epitaph is dreaded very much by Ross?
2. Ross becomes a guest lecturer at which university?
3. We know that Joey had a history of a serious disease like kidney stone. He also gets another ill-timed disease when his insurance cover runs out. Which disease?
4. Joey gets mistaken for being the owner of a sports car and actually enjoys the attention. What car was it?
5. Joey is in need of money but is way too proud to take it. So, what new 'game' is invented by Chandler to let Joey win some money?
6. Why doesn't Rachel like running with phoebe?
7. Where was Joey's beautiful roommate Janine originally from?
8. Who did Phoebe mistake Kenny the copy guy at Rachel's workplace for?
9. What weird thing did Ross do in preparation for his date with Monica's colleague, Hillary?
10. Chandler accuses Janine of changing the 'feel' of the apartment. What does he say Janine is making Joey and the apartment?
11. What is Joey's roommate Janine's profession?
12. In the thanksgiving dinner in season six, Monica's parents were invited and Rachel was in charge of the only dessert that she messed up. What dessert was she trying to make?
13. When Monica lets Rachel make the dessert for Thanksgiving, she ends up making a trifle that is half trifle and half shepherd's pie. What led to this blunder?
14. Rachel buys furniture from a well-known store but tells Phoebe that she got it from the flea market because Phoebe hates that store. Where did Rachel buy the furniture from?

15. Why did Joey and Janine break up?

16. Ross gets his Joke published in a renowned magazine but Chandler claims it to be his. Where was the Joke published?

17. Why did Joey get fired from the coffeehouse?

18. Who gets Joey's job at the coffeehouse back requesting Gunther?

19. Who was making porn movies using Phoebe's name?

20. When the girls were discussing who they would date among them, Phoebe picked Rachel. What reason did Phoebe give Monica for not choosing her?

21. What was the first song Ross learnt to play on his keyboard?

22. What was the essence of the published Joke, which Ross and Chandler were fighting over?

23. How much money did Ross receive for getting the Joke published?

24. Who did Phoebe accuse of being a pushover?

25. What according to Ross is a state of total awareness, in which you can be prepared for any danger?

Answers:

1. "Ross Geller Three divorces"
2. NYU
3. Hernia
4. A Porsche
5. "Cups"
6. She runs like an elephant
7. Australia
8. Ralph Lauren
9. Whitens his teeth shiny bright
10. Girly
11. Dancer
12. English trifle
13. Cookbook pages that had stuck together
14. Pottery Barn
15. Because she doesn't like hanging out with Monica & Chandler
16. Playboy
17. He closes the shop to go to an audition
18. Rachel
19. Ursula
20. That she is high maintenance
21. Barracuda
22. That Monkey was the doctor
23. 100$
24. Rachel
25. Unagi

The One About Season-6: Set-2

1. What did Monica gift Chandler on their first Valentine's Day?
2. Ross's dates a girl called Elizabeth Stevens in Season 6 who was a student of his and much younger to him. Who portrayed the character of her father?
3. In the sixth season, the names of the entire cast added Arquette to their names as shown in the opening credits of the season's premiere episode. What was the story behind it?
4. Name the short-lived cop show in which Joey has a starring role alongside a robot.
5. What does Joey misinterpret the charity auction as?
6. Which expensive item does Joey end up buying at the silent auction by misunderstanding how an auction works?
7. Why isn't Chandler able to buy the perfect ring immediately?
8. Rachel gets fed up with Bruce Willis's character Paul and breaks up with him. Why?
9. Who was left guarding Chandler's perfect ring for Monica?
10. Joey wanted his picture to end up on the laundry wall, it did go up but not the way he wanted. What was written under Joey's photo in the laundry wall?
11. After the fire, Rachel got to stay with Monica who was very eager to have someone in her new guest room. What did she dub this new room as?
12. Chandler had to take her friend Dana out for a dinner to get Joey an audition for a movie starring which famous actor?
13. While it was believed that fire in Rachel & Phoebe's apartment was caused by Phoebe's candles, the fire investigators found otherwise. What was the reason for the fire?
14. What does the Japanese word 'unagi' actually mean?

15. What is common between the two episodes "The One with the Princess Leia Fantasy" and in "The One Where Chandler Gets Caught"?

16. With her voice-only appearance, it makes season 6 the only season where this popular recurring character doesn't appear physically. Who are we talking about?

17. In the episode, The One That Could Have Been, Which does Phoebe work for as a banker & stock specialist?

18. In the alternative universe, what does Chandler imagines he would be doing if he had quit his job?

19. Name the character who can't cry no matter what?

20. What did Rachel notice to figure out that the woman in porn movies they were watching wasn't phoebe but her twin sister Ursula in it?

21. Why did a man ask phoebe for her autograph saying he is her biggest fan?

22. The view of Ross admitting that he still wants to get back with Rachel and both he & Rachel nudging each other, led to something unexpected, something that had never happened before?

23. Repeated attempts were made to elicit some emotion from Chandler. Why is Chandler accused of being dead inside by Joey?

24. What does Joey yell after learning that the cooking magazine's pages were stuck together?

25. Which actor won an Emmy for his performance as Paul Stevens?

Answers:

1. A sock puppet that Phoebe made.
2. Bruce Willis
3. Courtney Cox marrying David Arquette
4. Mac and C.H.E.E.S.E
5. Joey thought bidders were guessing an item's worth, like *price is right*
6. A Yatch
7. Because he had loaned his credit card to Joey
8. He gets very soft & emotional and keeps crying
9. Phoebe
10. "Son of a Bitch"
11. 'Hotel Monica'
12. Al Pacino
13. Rachel's hair iron
14. A freshwater eel
15. Only episodes where the cast members turn up to Central Perk and find their sofa occupied. This only happens two other times
16. Janice
17. Meryl Lynch
18. Wrote stories for The New Yorker
19. Chandler
20. A heart tattoo
21. Thinks of her as a Pornstar
22. Chandler crying
23. Chandler's never cries
24. "Chandler!"
25. Bruce Willis

The One About Season-7: Set-1

1. What did Monica's parent spent her wedding fund on?
2. Rachel and Chandler keep stealing cheesecakes, claiming that they were the most delicious cheesecakes that they had ever eaten. Who were these cheesecakes addressed to?
3. Which recipe that Monica desperately wanted got burnt in Phoebe's apartment fire?
4. According to Phoebe, where did her grandma get the recipe for from?
5. Name the band that Chandler wants to play at his and Monica's wedding?
6. Who tries to teach Joey sailing but ultimately gives up and adopts his way of sailing?
7. In *The One With Rachel's Book* which item makes Joey's duck ill?
8. Whose resume listed qualifications like "three years of painting houses" and "two whole summers at T.G.I. Friday's"?
9. Phoebe dates Kyle, who knows both Chandler and Ross -- from their basketball club. By what name nickname do we better remember him as?
10. What does Rachel bribe Joey with to stop picking up women with Tag, so that he would stop too?
11. Monica's mom arranged to get her wedding announced in the newspaper, finally we see a photo with Joey posing as Chandler in the announcement. Why was Chandler removed from his own wedding announcement picture?
12. Which movie were Joey and Ross watching when they fall asleep together on the couch becoming the 'Nap Partners'?
13. Why did Chandler dump her girlfriend from summer camp?

14. Paleontology section of the library is only used by students to make out or fool around; therefore Ross decides to defend the area. Why? .

15. What was the name of puppy that Phoebe sneaks into the apartment, forcing Chandler to confess that he is afraid of dogs?

16. Ross becomes adamant on completing the '50 States Game' before he let himself eat the Thanksgiving dinner. How many states was Ross able to write?

17. Frustrated & hungry, not being able to name all the 50 states, even after working until midnight, which state does he count twice to reach 50 states?

18. For whom did Ross buy a pretty pink bike?

19. Ross wants to rent a Christmas suit to surprise Ben but he couldn't get one later in the day, so he invents Santa's Tex-Mex friend. What was he called?

20. While lighting the Hanukkah candles. Phoebe and Rachel show up to watch, and Phoebe remarks, "I understand why Superman is here, but why is there a porcupine at the Easter Bunny's funeral?"

21. Who appears dressed as Superman to surprise Ben in Christmas?

22. Who had a pet Tarantula as a kid which was eaten by a cat, later killing the cat itself?

23. Rachel sees Chandler eating something delivered to their door, and so he lets her taste it. What item delivered from Mama's Little Bakery according was the best they had ever tasted?

24. What name had Joey given his Barcalounger which he doesn't like to be moved?

25. Monica is really upset with her parents and Jack, feeling guilty, decides to show her once and for all that he loves her just as much as Ross. How do he do that?

Answers:

1. A beach house
2. Mrs. Braverman
3. chocolate chip cookie recipe
4. Her French grandmother "Nestle Toulouse".
5. Swing Kings
6. Rachel
7. Rachel's face cream
8. Tag Jones
9. 'Hums While He Pees'
10. Ralph Lauren shirts
11. His inability to smile for a good picture.
12. Die hard
13. Because she had gotten fat
14. Ross' doctoral dissertation was kept here
15. Clunkers
16. Forty-six
17. Nevada
18. Phoebe
19. The Holiday Armadillo
20. Who was being referred to as an Easter Bunny? Chandler in Santa's costume
21. Joey
22. Rachel
23. cheesecake
24. Rosita
25. Gave his Porsche to Monica

The One About Season-7: Set-2

1. According to Phoebe she had completed all goals except for one. Which goal Phoebe couldn't complete before her thirtieth birthday?
2. Which character is shown to have bought a red MGB sports car and claims to be a sports car enthusiast?
3. What was Tag's birthday gift for Rachel that received a lot flak from her friends?
4. Whose goal was to meet Portuguese people, have the perfect kiss and going to sniper school before turning 30?
5. Who claims to be 1/16th Portuguese?
6. Ross says that he has a surprise for Monica and Chandler's wedding, and when they hear someone playing the bagpipes extremely badly across the street they realize that's the surprise. Why was Ross planning to play Bagpipes?
7. What does Monica fight Megan for at Kleinman's?
8. Monica figures out that Phoebe's grandma didn't have a secret recipe and where did she pick up the recipe from?
9. How does Monica get the band 'Swing Kings' back from Megan?
10. What award was Joey nominated for his return as Drake Ramoray in Days of Our Lives?
11. Rachel was part of sorority at college and partied all the time. What was the name of Rachel's sorority?
12. Rachel made out with a sorority sister during college played by Wynona Ryder. What was the name of the girl?

13. When asked if she has ever been in a sorority Phoebe says she's a "Thigh Mega Tampon" which was eventually shut down. Why was it shut down according to Phoebe?

14. While choosing a tuxedo for the wedding, Chandler finds a tuxedo that fits him well and wants to have it until Rachel tells him it belonged to an actress. Which actress?

15. Chandler & Monica go to visit Chandler's father who works as drag artist in Vegas. What was his professional name?

16. What did Joey steal and wear to be comfortable with his masculinity making him a man, but is also a bit slutty according to Phoebe?

17. Rachel was "Porsche-ing" (speeding) around much to Ross's annoyance and are pulled over by Officer Hanson for speeding - he also discovers that Rachel does not have a valid driving license. Rachel tries a little flirting to get out of the situation. What does Rachel call Officer Hanson?

18. What does Joey's famous co-star Richard Crosby in the World War 1 movie keeps doing much to his annoyance?

19. Which actor/actress wore a wig throughout the series as the producers believed that the hair was too short for the character. The only episodes where you see the real hair is in The One That Could Have Been. Who are we talking about?

20. Which is the only episode in the series to contain no one but only the 6 main characters?

21. Ross tells his students, that he originally came up with this idea when was bitten by a mosquito and had a dream (shown in the blackboard behind him). What idea does he claim to have come up with?

22. Name the Australian Olympic swimmer who appeared as an extra in Central Perk?

23. When Chandler is hiding out in his office at work, what is the name on his office door?

24. Who has the most birthday celebrations shown overall?

25. In the one where they all turn 30, Phoebe is revealed to be the oldest of the group is Phoebe (after learning she is a year older than she thought), then who is the youngest of the lot?

Answers:

1. Making up with her sister
2. Ross
3. A scooter
4. Phoebe
5. Joey
6. Because of Chandler's Scottish origin
7. Discounted Wedding Dress
8. a bag of Nestle Toll House cookies
9. In exchange for her beloved wedding dress
10. Soapie Award
11. Kappa Kappa Delta
12. Melissa
13. Regina Phalange died of alcohol poisoning.
14. Diane Keaton's
15. Helena Handbasket
16. Rachel's underwear
17. Officer Handsome
18. Spitting in his face for the sake of articulation
19. Lisa Kudrow
20. TOW Monica's thunder
21. Jurassic Park
22. Ian Thorpe
23. MIKE SMITH.
24. Rachel
25. Rachel

The One About Season-8: Set-1

1. Rachel didn't want everyone to know that the pregnancy test was hers, so phoebe falsely admits that she is the one who is pregnant and the father of the child is famous. Who did she say was the father of the child?

2. Chandler had been taking dancing lessons before the wedding. Why wasn't he able to do the wedding dance?

3. At Monica's wedding, Ross wants to sit with Mona, a girl from the restaurant, so he changes his table number. Where does he end up sitting?

4. Joey admits he has small feet but "rest of the body is fine". What was revealed to be Joey's shoe size?

5. What did the kids at Ross's table in the wedding accuse him of?

6. Why was Ross unable to Dance with Mona? Little girls wanted to dance with him hopping on his feet

7. Where did Ross and Mona have the picture that Mona wants to use as a holiday card, taken?

8. Who was charged with Meshuga Nuts and a movie "Doctor Do me a little" while checking out of the wedding hotel?

9. When Monica's curiosity gets the best of her, she decides to open a tiny wedding present before Chandler comes back. Opening the first gift led her to open the rest looking for a set. What did the first gift contain?

10. While Chandler went through hell to re-create the photos again thinking that he had lost the camera and his wedding photos along with it. Where were the original cameras all along?

11. Chandler thought that he had lost the cameras with his wedding photos, what did he and Ross decide to do save Chandler from Monica's wrath?

12. Joey tells Monica & Phoebe that he remembers someone spending the night with Rachel 1 month back. Although he didn't see who it was, he has something the guy left. What did the guy leave?

13. The infamous "Red sweater" that Joey found in his apartment caused a lot of confusion & embarrassment. Who was ultimately revealed to be its owner?

14. What does Joey end up doing whenever he hears one of his friends is pregnant and the father is unknown, lending the name to the episode?

15. Phoebe & Joey realize that they don't have keys to Chandler and Monica's apartment. Phoebe needs her guitar and Joey wants food. How did they get the superintendent Mr. Treeger to break the door down.

16. To what does **Ross say** "Wha-what? What!? Well, they should put that on the box!"?

17. The alias used that Joey used while sleeping with Rachel's friend Irene by telling her magic Europe story Ken Adams

18. Name of the mountain Joey used in his pick-up European sex

19. What is revealed to be Chandler's middle name?

20. Chandler blocks the promotion of Bob, who calls Chandler by a different name since 5-year? What does he call him?

21. What does Joey dress as in the season 8-Halloween party? As Chandler

22. Chandler and Ross arm wrestle to see who's toughest. It's a draw, but Chandler lets Ross win. Why?

23. Who does Monica & Phoebe fight over dumping and firing first but end up doing it together?

24. Who is the first guy Rachel goes out with after getting pregnant?

25. Which club did Ross, Will Colbert - an overweight kid and a foreign student start in school? I Hate Rachel Greene Club.

Answers:

1. James Brolin (Barbara Streisand's Husband)
2. Slippery Shoes
3. At the kids table
4. 7
5. Of Farting
6. Little girls wanted to dance with him hopping on his feet
7. Rockefeller Centre
8. Joey
9. A salt shaker
10. In Rachel's Bag
11. Gate-crash another wedding to take fake photos
12. "Red Sweater"
13. Ross
14. He ends up proposing them
15. Saying there's gas leak
16. Rachel mentions that condoms work 97% of the time.
17. Ken Adams
18. Mt. Tibidabo
19. Muriel
20. Toby
21. As Chandler
22. So he can impress Mona, his date.
23. Tim
24. Joey's co-actor Kash
25. I Hate Rachel Greene Club.

The One About Season-8: Set-2

1. I-hate-Rachel-club started a vicious rumor that even spread to other schools, even Chandlers. What was the rumor?

2. Rachel was a popular & mean girl in her high school days. She used to bully an overweight kid Will Colbert who later returns as an attractive adult in the show. Which actor made a guest appearance as the adult Will Colbert?

3. Name the Lincoln High foreign exchange student from Thailand who was part of "I-hate-Rachel-Club with Ross Geller & Will Colbert?

4. Rachel is quite upset hearing about the rumour spread by the 'club' until she's reminded that she also did spread some rumors about Ross making out with someone. What was the rumor?

5. Phoebe desperately tries to get tickets to a concert through Ben, who is in the same class as the celebrity's son. However, his wife Trudie does see that Phoebe is just using Ben to get tickets and kicks her out. Whose concert ticket was Phoebe after?

6. According to Joey, why is his youngest sister Dina, one of the smartest of the Tribbiani children?

7. Bobby Corso was a nice and funny guy but not too smart. He was in a gangsta rap band called Numbnuts with his friend, Rooster. Why was Joey mad at him?

8. Who does Monica hate for drunkenly urinating on their ice sculpture at their engagement party?

9. Why did Phoebe bring a random man named Roger to the apartment to meet Rachel during her pregnancy?

10. What was the late wedding present that Phoebe gave Chandler and Monica?

11. Why did Chandler's hand freeze in a claw shape?

12. Why did Monica and Phoebe have to play and beat all of Chandler's high scores before Ben comes over?

13. Joey is nervous by the new feelings towards Rachel which intensify when she asks him to hold her while watching a horror movie. Which Horror film were they watching?

14. Ross's new advanced paleontology class was 10 minutes away. He would always be late or too tired after reaching the class. How does he finally manage to find a way to make it to the advanced class easily and in time?

15. What were "Phoebe, Sandrine, Rain, James, Ruth, Helen, Isabella and Delilah" contenders for?

16. Joey has a dream about Rachel giving birth to his baby. What did the baby's face look like?

17. Why was Phoebe uncomfortable giving massages to Monica after the first time?

18. Joey is still depressed that he can't be with Rachel, so Phoebe gets him the happiest dog in the world to cheer him up. What was the name of the dog, (a very apt name considering Joey's food preferences)?

19. Phoebe dates a guy named Don who she thinks is Monica's soul-mate. Apart from Allesandro's being one his favourite restaurants, what dream do Monica and Don bond over?

20. Mona comes by Ross's apartment and picks up an item as something to remember him by which he rudely says no to. What did she want to keep?

21. Phoebe dates someone called Roger who was constantly cheerful, talkative, energetic and enthusiastic but with a strange and annoying habit. What did he do to irritate phoebe?

22. Joey auditions for a job as a game show host and Chandler and Ross help him practice by pretending to be the contestants. What was the name of the game?

23. Who did Phoebe and Monica forget to invite in Rachel's baby shower?

24. Who kept betting on Rachel's baby birth date?

25. Marc and Julie are a couple who shared the room with Rachel in Hospital. They had unusual nicknames for each other. What did they call each other?

26. Who lets Rachel have a name she had picked out for her own future children?

27. Which recurring character of the show was pregnant during the same time as Rachel?

28. Chandler and Monica think they are ready to have a baby, try to have unprotected sex in the hospital, but nurses & other people kept walking in on them. Where did they finally have sex?

29. Who discovers Chandler and Monica having sex and thinks they are doing it wrong and goes all over the hospital to get the folders on how to conceive a child, telling them some things they don't want to know in the process?

Answers:

1. She was a Hermaphrodite
2. Brad Pitt.
3. Ta-Taka-Ki-Kek
4. Ross made out with the 50-year old librarian
5. Sting
6. Because she took the S.A.Ts
7. He had got his sister Dina Pregnant
8. Chandler's Boss, Doug
9. To have sex with Rachel
10. The game Ms Pac-Man.
11. Playing the Pac-Man all day long
12. To erase the inappropriate initials Chandler had entered in the high scores
13. Cujo.
14. By wearing roller blades.
15. Emma's potential names
16. little baby Ross
17. She starts making sex noises
18. Mozzarella
19. That they both want to live in a house made of cheese.
20. His Pink Shirt
21. He made a big fuss about even the most trivial things.
22. Bamboozled
23. Rachel's mother Sandra Greene
24. Monica
25. "Evil Bitch" and "Sick Bastard"
26. "Emma"
27. Janice
28. In a Janitorial room.
29. Jack Geller

The One About Season-9: Set-1

1. What pie did Monica eat for the pie eating contest that she won in her 6th grade?

2. How much money did aunt Liddy usually give Monica & Chandler when she visited?

3. In which state did Phoebe plan to live a life of a soccer mom with Mike?

4. When Chandler notices that Joey has written a large check to Monica and asks Joey, what does he say Monica needed the money for?

5. Monica had organized a list of careers for Chandler alphabetically into files and folders. At the beginning of the list Chandler says "That's a great idea!". Which career did Monica start with?

6. Which actor plays the character of Phoebe's love interest Mike?

7. What does Rachel call Chandler after he told Monica he loved her breasts just the way they are?

8. Phoebe arranges for Rachel to go on blind date with a guy named Steve. By what nickname do we remember Steve as?

9. What does Joey try to get one of friend's first child named after to carry on his "family name"? (hint : Use some Joey Logic)

10. Who used to mug people on the streets?

11. What was the name of Ross's Comic book that was taken when he was mugged as a child?

12. Why didn't Mike want to get married again?

13. What did Chandler post about Ross on their college's alumni website?

14. Why did Phoebe drop the lottery tickets off the balcony?

15. Chandler is initially upset when the open positions for the assistant are filled up but as it out turns they offered him a better position. Which position was Chandler offered by the ad agency?

16. Despite losing half of the lottery tickets, the group still wins some money. How much did they win?

17. Ross was invited to Paleontology convention as a keynote speaker, so his friends also tag along. Where was it happening?

18. Who accidentally erases Ross's keynote speech resulting in Ross and Charlie staying up all night together to rebuild it?

19. Rachel and Joey don't get most of what Ross is saying but both giggle over a term. Which term are we talking about?

20. Monica and Mike get into a competitive match at Barbados. Which game were they playing?

21. What was the name of Emma's pediatrician that makes Joey chuckle every time he hears it?

22. When Chandler changes the channel quickly on seeing Monica in Tulsa, what does Monica think Chandler gets off to?

23. Why was Chandler very jealous of one of Monica's co-workers Jeffery?

24. Which 'friend' still visited his old pediatrician (Dr. Gettleman)?

25. What was the name of the male nanny that Rachel and Ross hired to care for Emma?

Answers:

1. Blueberries
2. Five dollars
3. Connecticut
4. For a Boob Job
5. Advertising
6. Paul Rudd
7. Fascist
8. The Stoned guy
9. As "Joey"
10. Phoebe
11. "Science Boy"
12. Due to his first failed marriage
13. That he is dead
14. Frightened by a pigeon
15. Junior Copywriter
16. Three dollars
17. Barbados
18. Chandler
19. "Homo-Erectus."
20. ping-pong
21. Dr. Weiner.
22. Shark documentaries.
23. Chandler tries to prove he's funnier.
24. "Rossy"
25. Sandy

The One About Season-9: Set-2

1. How does Joey learn his life lessons from Emma's nanny?
2. Which adult song from *Sir Mix-a-Lot* does Ross sing to make Emma laugh for the first time?
3. Which bird farm did Joey consider investing his money in?
4. What do Joey and Chandler find in Richard's apartment?
5. What is the condition for Chandler getting Emma in case Ross and Rachel die?
6. Name Chandler's coworker who makes a pass at him on Christmas?
7. Phoebe was nervous and couldn't properly perform her role as a nurse so Joey had a talk with the director. When Phoebe asked him what the director said, what does he replace the bad 'F' word with?
8. What is Chandler's Job description?
9. Who had an Internet Company that went under and lost an ear in a boating accident?
10. Chandler types in Ross's mail "Also, I cloned a _____ in my lab. She is now my girlfriend. I don't care what society says about it, it's the best sex I ever had...and send". What's fills the blank?
11. How did Ross die according to Chandler on the alumni website?
12. What did Ross post about Chandler on the Alumni's newsroom?
13. Name of the ex-boyfriend that Ross makes up when he slips up that Phoebe never had a long serious relationship?

14. Joey bought tickets for one woman to prevent the rest of the gang coming to the Soap Opera Party. What was the title of the play?

15. What did Chandler try to bring Monica form Vermont?

16. What was Phoebe's weapon of choice during her mugging days?

17. Who did Tom Gordon come to visit on seeing the news about Chandler & Ross on the college's alumni website?

18. Who said, "Trust me, when it comes to psychology I know what I'm talking about! I took two psych classes in college"?

19. What made Ross get excited about going to the inn with Chandler?

20. Who claims to have come up with the line "Got Milk" first?

21. What did the sticker on Ross's backpack during the mugging say?

22. What was written on Phoebe's box of stuff she got from mugging people?

23. What was the name of Phoebe's rat friend?

24. What type of new sneakers was Chandler trying hard to come up with a sales pitch for?

25. Who did Chandler and Monica run into Janice at the fertility clinic?

Answers:

1. Through puppet shows.
2. "Baby Got Back"
3. Emu Farm
4. A tape with Monica written on it
5. If Monica is alive
6. Wendy
7. Puppy
8. Statistical Analysis and Data Reconfiguration
9. Andrea Rich
10. Dinosaur
11. Hit by a blimp
12. That he's gay
13. Vikram
14. 'Why Don't You Like Me?'
15. Maple Candy
16. A pipe
17. Chandler
18. Monica
19. moonlit boat rides
20. Ross
21. Geology Rocks
22. Crap from the street
23. Bob
24. "slorps" – sneakers with wheels
25. Janice

The One About Season-10: Set-1

1. What are the names of Chandler and Monica's children?
2. What was the name of Phoebe's painting?
3. Who did Chandler & Monica adopt the kids from?
4. Which famous actor appeared as Roy Goodbody, the stripper hired on Phoebe's bachelorette party?
5. Who teaches or more like tries to teach Joey French?
6. Which European city was Rachel planning to move in the final season?
7. Ross managed to convince Rachel's boss at Ralph Lauren to make her a new job offer by bribing him with something. What did he bribe him with?
8. Phoebe didn't have anyone to walk her down the aisle, so one of the guys had to do it. Do you remember who?
9. Where did Monica & Chandler move?
10. In The One Where The Stripper Cries, what game show does Joey appear on as a contestant?
11. When Phoebe changes her name to "Princess Consuela" Mike also changed his name to teach her a lesson. What was Mike's new name?
12. To whom does Phoebe say these following words "You've sort of been like a dad to me. You know, you look out for me and share your wisdom."?
13. Why did Mike had to visit a doctor after his honeymoon with Phoebe?
14. How did Joey start his recommendation letter to the adoption agency?

15. What was the name of the 8-year-old little girl who convinced Joey to let go of his friends?

16. Why didn't Rachel want Emma to play with swings in the park?

17. Rachel & Phoebe see Chandler getting into a car with a blonde stranger and coming out 'pretty happy' and assume that he is having an affair. Who was the blonde lady?

18. Where did Rachel get the cowgirl outfit for Emma's baby beauty pageant?

19. Who did Rachel want to play her in the movie, if a movie is made about a swing incident?

20. What name does Phoebe allow her friends to call her instead of Princess Consuela?

21. What is the significance of 'CRW-33815-D' in Chandler & Monica's life?

22. Who had Chandler kissed during the freshman year party at the college?

23. Whose real father could be an all American football player, or the convicted murderer who killed his father with a shovel?

24. Rachel met someone named Mr. Campbell for her lunch interview with which company?

25. While moving her stuff out of Ralph Lauren Rachel meets her old colleague Mark who informs her about a potential opening at his new company. Where was he working then?

Answers:

1. Jack & Erica Bing
2. Gladys
3. Erica
4. Danny DeVito
5. Phoebe
6. Paris
7. Dinosaur stuff
8. Chandler
9. Westchester County
10. Pyramid
11. Crapbag
12. Joey
13. He didn't poop the whole time he was there
14. "Dear baby adoption __ __." FITB
15. Mackenzie
16. She was stuck in a swing when she was 4 years old.
17. Nancy, the realtor
18. Joey's Cabbage Patch Kid
19. Claire Danes
20. Valerie
21. Their adoption file
22. Rachel
23. The Bing children
24. Gucci
25. Louis Vuitton

The One About Season-10: Set-2

1. Who pretends to be Estelle on the phone to avoid telling Joey that Estelle had died?

2. Who didn't receive a special goodbye from Rachel at her Going Away Party?

3. What was Joey's final reply when he was urged to choose between sex or food?

4. How many rigged coin tosses did Joey lose to Rachel when he was trying to stop Rachel from going to Paris by winning a coin toss?

5. Why did Joey & Chandler have to break the foosball table?

6. Who got Emma's ear pierced?

7. When Phoebe asks Monica, where did she go to get her name changed, what was her reply?

8. Which budding actor in the final season can now be seen in a starring role in the psychological thriller drama series The Alienist?

9. What did they all do before saying their final goodbye to Monica's apartment?

10. Who hadn't lived in Monica's apartment during the entire series?

11. What did Ross find in Rachel's dad's refrigerator which he thinks might have solved the mystery around his heart attack?

12. Which actress played the role Erica, the woman who let Monica and Chandler adopt her babies?

13. What did Phoebe say Emma won the trophy at?

14. Chandler wrote a song the night he saw Ross kissing Adrienne Turner, although he and Ross both made a pact that neither one of them would date her. What was the name of the song?

15. Who turned out to be Monica's "midnight mystery kisser" at the college freshman year party?

16. Monica & Chandler got everyone gifts to make them feel a little better before sharing the news of their moving out of the city. Joey's bag was white with red dots on it. What did it contain?

17. When Chandler gets the adoption interview call, Joey says "I went through the exact same thing with Alicia Mae Emory…The waiting, the wondering…then one day, I get that call from Toys "R" Us…she was in stock!". What was he talking about?

18. When one of Mike's groomsmen can't make it, who does Mike decide to replace the missing groomsmen with?

19. Who officiated Mike & Phoebe's wedding?

20. Why did Phoebe's wedding ceremony have to be cut short?

21. Whose toy wins the toy race held on Emma's Birthday?

22. What was the shape of the cake Rachel received from the bakery for Emma's birthday?

23. What was supposed to be the original shaped of the cake Rachel ordered for Emma's birthday?

24. What was the toy race used to decide at Emma's party?

25. Joey's emotional reading of which piece brought them all on the verge of tears?

DO ME A SOLID: IF YOU LIKE IT RATE IT, SHARE IT, REVIEW IT

Your support and ratings helps us continue producing good content.

Please mail me your feedback, ideas and topics for the next edition or a new trivia theme altogether

@

donaldblake.trivia@gmail.com

Answers:

1. Phoebe
2. Ross
3. "I want girls on bread"
4. 57 in a row
5. Duck and chick got stuck inside the table
6. Amy
7. The Ministry of Names Bureau
8. Dakota Fanning (Mackenzie)
9. Kept their keys on table
10. Ross
11. Bacon and heavy cream
12. Anna Faris
13. Spelling Bee
14. Betrayal in the common room
15. Ross
16. A meatball sub.
17. The Cabbage Patch Kid
18. Chappy, Mike's Dog
19. Joey
20. Chappy's heart rate was slowing way down
21. Joey's
22. A phallus shaped
23. A bunny with Emma's face on it
24. Who gets to leave
25. "Love You Forever"

Printed in Great Britain
by Amazon